Can Bill Sob? No!
and
Len in the Hot Sun

PHASE 2

Level 2 – Red

Helpful Hints for Reading at Home

The graphemes (written letters) and phonemes (units of sound) used throughout this series are aligned with Letters and Sounds. This offers a consistent approach to learning whether reading at home or in the classroom.

HERE IS A LIST OF PHONEMES FOR THIS PHASE OF LEARNING. AN EXAMPLE OF THE PRONUNCIATION CAN BE FOUND IN BRACKETS.

Phase 2			
s (sat)	a (cat)	t (tap)	p (tap)
i (pin)	n (net)	m (man)	d (dog)
g (go)	o (sock)	c (cat)	k (kin)
ck (sack)	e (elf)	u (up)	r (rabbit)
h (hut)	b (ball)	f (fish)	ff (off)
l (lip)	ll (ball)	ss (hiss)	

HERE ARE SOME WORDS WHICH YOUR CHILD MAY FIND TRICKY.

Phase 2 Tricky Words			
the	to	I	no
go	into		

TOP TIPS FOR HELPING YOUR CHILD TO READ:

• Allow children time to break down unfamiliar words into units of sound and then encourage children to string these sounds together to create the word.

• Encourage your child to point out any focus phonics when they are used.

• Read through the book more than once to grow confidence.

• Ask simple questions about the text to assess understanding.

• Encourage children to use illustrations as prompts.

This book focuses on the phonemes /l/ and /ll/ and is a red level 2 book band.

Can Bill Sell It?
and
Len in the Hot Sun

Written by
Robin Twiddy

Illustrated by
Danielle Webster-Jones

Can you say this sound and draw it with your finger?

Can Bill Sell It?

Written by
Robin Twiddy

Illustrated by
Danielle Webster-Jones

Bill is at the till.

Can Bill sell a mug?

Tap tap on the till.

Bill did sell a mug.

Bill is at the till.

Can Bill sell a doll?

Tap tap on the till.

Bill did sell a doll to Sal.

Bill is at the till.

Can Bill sell a tub of mud?

Tap tap on the till.

Bill did sell the tub of mud to a pig.

Can you say this sound and draw it with your finger?

Len In the Hot Sun

Written by
Robin Twiddy

Illustrated by
Danielle Webster-Jones

Len is in the hot sun.

Len is hot in the hot sun.

Len got a red leg in the hot sun.

Rub the leg, Len. Rub it in the hot sun.

Len is at the log hut.

The hut is in the hot sun.

It is not hot in the hut.

But Len is not in the hut.

Len is in the hot sun.

Len is hot in the hot sun.

The log hut has a hot lock.

Len is red in the hot sun.

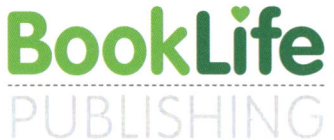

©2022 **BookLife Publishing Ltd.**
King's Lynn, Norfolk, PE30 4LS, UK

ISBN 978-1-80155-802-0

All rights reserved. Printed in Poland.
A catalogue record for this book is available from the British Library.

Can Bill Sell It? and Len in the Hot Sun
Written by Robin Twiddy
Illustrated by Danielle Webster-Jones

An Introduction to BookLife Readers...

Our Readers have been specifically created in line with the London Institute of Education's approach to book banding and are phonetically decodable and ordered to support each phase of Letters and Sounds.

Each book has been created to provide the best possible reading and learning experience. Our aim is to share our love of books with children, providing both emerging readers and prolific page-turners with beautiful books that are guaranteed to provoke interest and learning, regardless of ability.

BOOK BAND GRADED using the Institute of Education's approach to levelling.

PHONETICALLY DECODABLE supporting each phase of Letters and Sounds.

EXERCISES AND QUESTIONS to offer reinforcement and to ascertain comprehension.

BEAUTIFULLY ILLUSTRATED to inspire and provoke engagement, providing a variety of styles for the reader to enjoy whilst reading through the series.

AUTHOR INSIGHT:
ROBIN TWIDDY

Robin Twiddy is one of BookLife Publishing's most creative and prolific editorial talents, who imbues all his copy with a sense of adventure and energy. Robin's Cambridge-based first class honours degree in psychosocial studies offers a unique viewpoint on factual information and allows him to relay information in a manner that readers of any age are guaranteed to retain. He also holds a certificate in Teaching in the Lifelong Sector, and a postgraduate certificate in Consumer Psychology.

A father of two, Robin has written over 70 titles for BookLife and specialises in conceptual, role-playing narratives which promote interaction with the reader and inspire even the most reluctant of readers to fully engage with his books.

This book focuses on the phonemes /l/ and /ll/ and is a red level 2 book band.